Song of the PHOENIX

Munazza Arif

First Published in June 2021

ISBN: 978-93-5427-564-7

BLUEROSE PUBLISHERS

www.bluerosepublishers.com

info@bluerosepublishers.com

+91 8882 898 898

Cover Design:

Joshua Freitas

Typographic Design:

Namrata Saini

Distributed by: BlueRose, Amazon, Flipkart, Shopclues

DEDICATION

"For Amma and Abba, who made me see the world through books. My daughter Asna, who brought out the best in me. My husband Arif, who bore with my mooning in between conversations and to all those who encouraged me."

AUTHOR'S NOTE

ME ON MYSELF

Like a narcissus by the river
Now I should look into the mirror
Reflect and write what I see
My doppelgänger or is it me?
Round-faced , hair long and black
A woman stares at me back
Where is that girl with all the dreams
To change the world by her steam
Lost in the world of books
Cared not much about her looks
When I came as a bride
Many dreams did I hide
My family duties bound me down
In its rigorous cycle I bogged down
Time flew my duties grew
Never thought of my hobby new
Would dream of poetry often
Would ignore on waking then
Now at this life's bend
I tried to give it a hand
Never thought it will be liked
I wrote and tried to hide
I thank God for his bounties and Gifts
I wish my focus doesn't shift
Thanks everyone ten times nine
For appreciating my lines

BY MUNAZZA

I have written this book after crossing many hurdles of my own mind. The very first difficulty was that I was not too sure of myself, if I would be able to do it. I would write my poems and hide them, never showing them to anyone. Maybe I was afraid of rejection and ridicule. I was writing them for myself, just to express what I felt.

On my daughter's coaxing I shared some on social media platforms. After receiving an encouraging response there and with the help of Bluerose Publishers, I took the first step towards publishing my book.

Characters I have spun are fictitious but you will surely identify with their stories as ones happening around you. My journey has begun. Let's see where the way will lead me Thanks to the Almighty and everyone who gave me a helping hand.

- Munazza Arif

SONG OF THE PHOENIX

PROLOGUE

Geeta woke up with a start. Her nightmares were back again. It had been a while since she had had them. She looked at her bedside clock it was 3 o' clock in the morning or night, whatever you may say It was still dark and the sun was yet to come up It is strange how when you are already awake, things don 't seem so dark but when you wake up from sleep at night, everything appears pitch dark. That 's your mind playing tricks I guess.

The scene played in her mind again.

She was running and running in an unknown place, on a dark road - running for her life or running from someone she always tried not to think of. She tried to remember some details but all she could feel was fear

Her dream always ended with a gun being pointed at her.

She always tried hard to recollect details, was it her subconscious warning her of what was coming?

Was it symbolic of her anxiety or was it a past-life dream?

Dreams always have the quality to take you where you have never been or muddle up places you have been to.

People say that when you go to sleep, a tiny fragment of your soul leaves your body to roam around the world and then comes back to you

MIND

The journey of mind is strange

It can take a fanciful flight

Travel at the speed of light

Or it can stay put at a place

It doesn't stick to our body's pace

Can make us a prisoner or liberate,

It can trouble us or can sate

Mind has an identity of its own.

But what had triggered them now after all these years? Geeta thought and looked around at the light of the lamppost filtering through the crevices of her window.

Now the room didn't look so dark and scary. It was normal.

However, I couldn' t sleep anymore. She was wide awake. It had always been like that. She had never been able to sleep after the nightmares.

"I should better make use of my time", she thought and opened her laptop, the light from the laptop screen brightening the area around her. There were some emails.

But it was only one mail that caught her attention.

She knew now that she had to make a decision.

SONG OF THE PHOENIX

Chapter-1

Oh God! Don't let this happen, do not let me miss the bus, I prayed fervently as my taxi zoomed towards the bus stop.The bus was standing there as if waiting for me.

I quickly got down with my backpack and rushed towards my bus; to embark on a journey I had not thought would be a life changer. My life had been humdrum for quite some time now.

HUMDRUM LIFE

My humdrum life - same routine, same strife
Is it a boon or bane?
It will make me mad; maybe sane
Should I be thankful for God's gifts
Or wait for a paradigm shift

I had not been out on vacation for years. After seeing that mail on my laptop, it was as if a bulb had lit in my mind. I had concluded I needed a solo trip to introspect and start living again. I had made the decision on the spur of the moment and had informed my boss that I was taking my overdue leave and should be contacted only if something important came up.

She had understood, and approved my leave as long as I submitted my projects by deadline.

I knew that if I did not do anything now I would become almost invisible - just like a piece of furniture - necessary, but unnoticed.

I wanted something new in my life.

The nightmares were back once more and on top of that, the goddamn email had triggered my anxiety attack again.

ANXIETY STORY

Let me tell you my anxiety story:
I would imagine all scenarios gory,
Worry to the hilt inane,
Driving myself insane
Some thought it was just drama and ruse
But was triggered by past trauma and abuse
It was affecting my work,
Duties I began to shirk
My counsellor helped me in my plight
Made me relax and feel alright.

My counsellor had asked me several times to go on a vacation and relax.

However, I had always ignored and put it off for later

Geeta was a pretty woman of 34 , working in a media company. She was also a writer and poet. Quite smart to look at, she had shoulder- length raven black hair and an impeccable dusky complexion with sharp features. Her main assets were her beautiful eyes, fringed with long, dark lashes.

She had no idea how expressive her eyes were. All of her 5'4" slim and athletic frame added to her attractiveness and charisma. She was oblivious to her own charm and as a result, had lost confidence and faith in herself.

Sometimes all you need is validation and love from people and know that you are beautiful and are important to them.

Outwardly she was doing okay, but she was fighting her own demons.

She would often muse about her anxiety and pain. That day it was drizzling when she had returned home from her office. The weather had made the house look lonelier and gloomy. Getting wet in the rain she had sobbed.

THE DOOR KNOB

Getting drenched in rain
Eases my pain
My heart with ache throbs
Silently it bears and quietly it sobs
Have I turned into a door knob?
Always there, noticed by none
Will be realised when broken
Then I guess it will be too late
They will be left out of the gate

:————x———:

I was wallowing in self-pity again. I had to reprimand myself. I knew it was not good for my mental health. I had decided to take the matter in my hands. My counsellor's advice and that mail I had received, had spurred my speed of finally making a decision.

Was there a connection between the nightmares and the mail? I wondered aloud. Only time would tell, but for now, my destination was decided. McLeod Ganj, it would be.

I quickly booked the tickets to avoid any change of mind. I also booked a backpackers' hostel, packed my shoes, a few of my things and I was ready.

Here now in the bus, I looked around at the passengers. I just laid a cursory glance on them and settled down on my seat. The seat next to me was empty, no one had come to occupy it yet.

"Hi! I am Sumi". A voice jolted me from my musings.

I looked at the outstretched hand and the smiling dark eyes of a young girl.

She seemed to be in her late twenties or mid you could say, in Denims, with a smile on her lips and glasses on her eyes. They kind of suited her.

"Geeta!", I reluctantly replied as if imparting something precious to a stranger.

She settled down on her seat, joy and enthusiasm eminent in every gesture.

I looked around at the other passengers An old couple seated two seats ahead seemed to be busy in discussion about their kids or other family matters A newly-wed couple was seated a few rows in front One can always make them out ,how they seem to be lost in their own world and have no eyes for anyone else ; besides, the wife was wearing choodas – the red and white bangles newly-wed women wear.

Then there were three young girls who seemed to have decided to take a hiatus from work and go on a trip

TRIP

Three young ladies

Out on a trip

Lovely smart and hip

Having the time of their life

After days of sweat and strife

————x————:

The bus had started to move and it was evening already.

The sky was a wonderful combination of crimson and blue – violet dusk was descending.

Twilight was my favourite part of the day. I loved watching sunsets, the way the sky showed different patterns and colours. It appealed to my soul.

THE TWILIGHT

The twilight when it is half light

Sun is deciding to rest

Colouring the sky bright red with its heart blood

This time is the best

when birds fly home to nest

At twilight the day looks inside

At the dark spots which the sun hides

It retrospects before it dies

:————x————:

I was already feeling a sense of uplift.

CHAPTER-2

My eyes scanned the bus again. There was one gentleman maybe in his forties as I could only guess by looking at his back and he was busy on his laptop.

On his side was a monk clad in his traditional maroon attire looking out of the window. Two boys who looked like college students may be coming from the hostel.

The lady behind me was perhaps a bakery owner, talking to her employees on the phone, instructing them about ovens and a cake delivery.

How strange is the human mind? It processes everything it sees and hears, relevant or irrelevant and presents them to us when needed, like Dev Patel in Slumdog Millionaire answering all of Anil Kapoor's questions adeptly.

"Want some?", Sumi offered a packet of chips.

"No no! It's ok, you have it", I replied.

"Please don't hesitate. I have more if you like. You can have some cookies too! Actually I never travel without my supply of food. You never know when you need it", she chirped.

The bus was traversing through the streets of Delhi.

Delhi. My beautiful Delhi.

A strange attraction this place holds, if you have been here once you would want to come again.

But here I was, running away from it to wipe away some cobwebs.

Have you ever travelled in a bus? When you look out, everyone seems below you. It is a strange feeling. On Sumi 's insistence I picked a few chips from her packet but you know how chips are like peanuts and you just can 't stop at one!

"I love to talk! I can't sit still. You seem to be the silent type", Sumi quipped.

I pondered.

SILENT

***S**ometime people struggle*

***I**n their minds*

***L**et no one know they're*

***E**ncountering devils*

***N**ot knowing what to do*

***T**hey keep mum*

:————x————:

Night was descending and the bus was now on a highway moving with speed. I was relaxed. Sumi began speaking again. She was an MBA who worked as an HR at some firm in Delhi and lived In a flat shared with her friends.

I answered her inquiries in monosyllables. She's so inquisitive, I reflected

WO WER WAS?

When, where, who, what?

Questions questions quite a lot

Love laughter lives lost

Sum of all answers sought

:————x————:

Sumi took out a Sunday newspaper and began solving crosswords. At long last my interest was piqued and I started craning my neck towards the newspaper.

CROSSWORDS

Do you like crosswords? She asked
Oh! I love them, was my answer
I wait for my Sunday paper
With pen in hand
Taxing my brain
My head buried like an ostrich in sand
Feel elated when a clue I solve
Then to next I proceed with resolve,
When stuck I am snappy
Isn't life like crosswords
So many crossroads black and white at places
You have to fill appropriate spaces,
Sometimes dull sometimes zappy
Whatever, crosswords make me happy

:————x————:

The ice between us was broken. We both were now busy solving crosswords.

She was equally good at it. Once that was finished, she started reading all the news and some of the interesting entertainment news she read a bit aloud.

CHAPTER-3

Sumi and I were soon engaged in small talk, topics like feminism ,current affairs and more. She had her own point of view on every topic and I thought that she was immature and had not seen much of life's ways, that's why she seemed so chirpy.

"You seem like a tortured soul!", She blurted with a hint of sympathy in her voice.

"What is your story?"; I was startled. Sumi was looking at me with questioning eyes. "You seem to be running away from someone or something", she continued.

I looked at her. "Not everyone has a story", I told her.

"I don't believe you. You yourself told me that you are a poet. Life's painful experiences make you a poet", she said wisely.

I had no argument against that. Wasn't this what we have been hearingfor ages?

STORIES

Everyone has a story
Of their own
Some we know
Some unknown
Some tell in the guise of fiction
While some do it with conviction
Stories of love, separation and pain
Unbelievable story of grit and gains

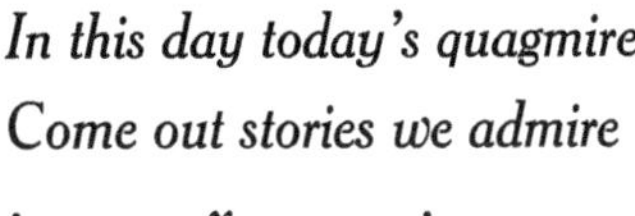

In this day today's quagmire
Come out stories we admire

:————x————:

"My HR training and my job has taught me enough to read between the lines."

THE LANGUAGE

Your lips are mum
Eyes are guarded
Trying to hide secrets
Is in vain
Your language of body
Reveals it plain

:—————x————:

"Who was he or she who hurt you? I know I am a complete stranger but you don't have to tell me names or designations, just vent your heart out I will tell no tales as I do not know you any more than a person who crossed my path for just a few hours I can sense you are hurting from inside", she said and stopped. Her dark eyes were fixed on my face. Waiting for an answer.

LUCIFER

He was handsome appeared kind,
With his talks he would blind
Monster he was when behind
A con man from every angles
After all Lucifer is the most beautiful of angels

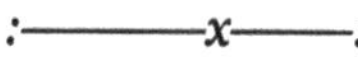

Sumi looked at me seriously through her glasses, as I answered ambiguously. I had thought so. She had hit bang on spot but I had my own misgivings. I always had trouble opening up and moreover she was a stranger who I had met only moments ago. Yes, many people have a habit of venting their heart out with all and sundry but I was not one of them. I wished I was. Then I won't be carrying so much baggage. But It is hard to be what you are not.

A lot of unlearning is required to offload. So I decided to turn the conversation towards other topics of global nature.

REWILDING

Rewilding is the need of the time
In order to save some species prime
Man's lust for blood and hunt
Animals had to bear the brunt
He encroached upon the woods
Only thought of his selfish good
Animals' number started to shrink

Some are on extinction brink
Forgetting what you give comes back to you
First it is them then next will be you
Cutting trees is drawing earth 's blood
Cities are faced with worst of floods
Planting more trees and growing jungle
Is only the way out of this bungle
Rewilding of animals who are less in number
Will be atonement for our blunders

CHAPTER-4

Sumi however returned to the previous topic. I think she was trying to process everything and had caught me side-tracking the issue

She shook her head and exclaimed "Oh I got it !The Venus flytrap!"

"Venus flytrap?", I stuttered.

"Yes !"

I had read this poem and it summed up some of the relationships I had seen. Some of my colleagues fit the bill. Maybe you will see what I mean in the next lines.

THE VENUS FLYTRAP

Some men are like Venus flytrap
Waiting for women to fall in their lap
Attracting them with looks and lies
Women get trapped like vulnerable flies
Then they suck their life force
Leaving them listless in due course
The fly then realises its errors
She has landed in a house of horrors
Where she will be the breadwinner and maid- in-hand
Will be raped and punished by this fiend
Many a guy I know of this type
Who are nothing but hype
Although they have trapped a fly

Still they wait for others on the sly
They stand tall as if they are king
But in reality they are finks
So girls be clever and be smart
Don't fall for such unsavoury tarts
They are actually losers and weak
So they try to be control freak
The same holds for Guys too
Who are attracted to the goo
In the guise of flowers and honey
They fall for girls after their money
When they have taken them as mate
They realise their error much too late
Be wary of smooth talkers with oodles of charm
They might cause you and your heart great harm
So guys and girls always see red flags
Before you commit to forever hashtag

:————x————:

I stared at her astuteness. I was at a loss of words. She was an intelligent, observant girl with uncanny knowledge about human nature at this young age. But age has never been a sign of maturity or experience, you can be old with lack of maturity and experience and sometimes life teaches you various things within a short span of your time on earth. Now I was looking at her differently.

For the first time I looked at her closely and not cursorily.

She was a tall girl with a wheatish skin tone, a roundish oval face, dark brown eyes with glasses on and a cute round nose. Her smiling lips with perfect teeth complimented her face further.

She was neither too slim nor too fat Clad in a denim jacket, jeans and a white top with some kind of a locket hanging from a chain on her neck, she exuded confidence.

Confidence is what matters. It makes you beautiful In this wide world of God's everything creation is beautiful.

Tarun had killed my confidence by calling me ugly ,dumb and a good-for-nothing thus filling me with self- doubt. That was a way of his , to control me I doubt if he ever loved me. I thought,

ES ESTE AMOR?

Love should free you ,
Not bind
Should not control you ,
With mind
Love lets you,
What you want to be
It doesn't bind,
Let's you free
Love should not be a prison
Heart has its own reasons

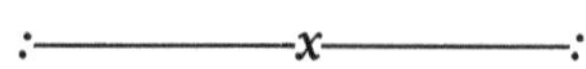

I jerked my head back to the present. I didn't want to think about that jerk

MASKS

People wear masks
They hide their true selves
Sometimes to save themselves from hurt
Sometimes to save others from hurt
Many times to hurt others
Often to con
Now mask is compulsory to don
What an irony?

I started looking out of the window to break my train of thoughts. Meanwhile, the bus was running, honking, overtaking vehicles on the road. It was dark now outside.

CHAPTER-5

I wanted to know more about Sumi. She seemed like an interesting person to me Before delving into that corner of my heart where I shuddered to go,

I wanted to know her story, who she was and what made her tick.

In her own words everyone had a story and people spoke out of their own experiences. She must have been having a tale to tell too.

But we were approaching Karnal and the bus conductor had announced that we would be stopping there for a short while. Whoever wanted to freshen up could get down and do so.

The bus stopped. It was a dhaba on a highway Many passengers started to get down as the whole night journey was ahead. Sumi and I decided to get down as well.

Many other buses too had stopped there. There was quite a rush at the loo.

Sumi asked me if I wanted something to eat since she was going to get herself some food. She saw the hesitation on my face and said, "You can pay me on the bus. What do you want ?".

"Ok ! bring whatever you want", I told her.

"Oh man, exercise your choice don't let others decide.You are not a log or plant".

Those words struck a chord

"Samosa", came out of my mouth.

She nodded her head and went off in the other direction.

By that time I had freshened up and now I occupied a seat. I slightly turned my head to have a look at our bus, if it was indeed there. Satisfied that the bus was there, I sat down. Sumi too had returned with samosas for me and chola bhatura for herself.

We were busy eating and started discussing various current affairs.
Suddenly I popped the question out of the blue.

"Sumi, have you ever been in love ?"

She became quiet and thoughtful instantly.

I asked again, "Do you know what love is ? Have you ever…?"

"Yeah, I know, I have had this malady.

It rips your heart out."

THE MALADY

Love is a malady of the heart
You wake up from sleep with a start
Pines and yearns
Heart never learns
It is a thing so abstract
You know not when trapped
It's like waves of the ocean
Sometimes at crest, at passion's best
Other moment crashes by the beach
Just now with you, then out of reach
Crying and yearning for what it was
For that beautiful moment, if it could pause
:————x————:

I stared at her. We had finished our food. So we got up to go. Just as I stepped out in the open, my heart started to beat fast and I broke into perspiration.

Our bus was not there. A vacant space was staring back at us.

I rushed forward like a mad woman looking for the bus hoping that maybe it's hidden from my sight and has been parked at some other place.

"Ma'am the bus left a few minutes ago", a man standing there apprised.

"Oh my God! my luggage was in it!"

I was here, standing at a dhaba on Karnal highway, in the middle of the night.

My anxiety returned in full force. I started running after the bus as if I would be able to catch it on foot.

"Geeta ! Geeta ! Wait!"

Impervious to Sumi's calls I kept running - a lone woman running on an empty road at night.

After a while I came to my senses. I had come far on the dark, empty road I looked around on both sides of the road, there were trees and fields and darkness all around.

Now a different kind of fear engulfed me. The nightmare I kept having and my reality seemed to meld, I turned back.This time I started running in the direction of the dhaba and then suddenly, I halted in my tracks.

Standing in front of me, was Sumi.

With a very serious expression and a gun in her hand pointed towards me.

What a sight it would have been- two young women, in the middle of the night, on a lone deserted road , one pointing a gun at the other.

:————————x————————:

TERROR

"Why I was such a dumb ass
Who trusted this unknown lass"
Has everyone a motive whom we meet
That's why they come and talk sweet
I have committed a grave error
To land myself in this terror"

CHAPTER-6

Over the next few seconds, thousands of thoughts crossed my mind. Who is she? Is she a member of some gang ? Or has someone sent her to kill me?

The last thought was like a matchstick striking to fire in the dark. After that mail I had received, this actually seemed appropriate.

"Who are you?"

I hissed.

"Has Tarun sent you to kill me !?"

FEAR

Fear can make you brave
Or you can just cave
You can be the boss
Or can be led to the cross
Fear is the key
Between controlled and in control

Shut up Geeta!

In my anxiety I hadn't given a thought to my safety. A woman running around in an unknown place at midnight, was a lame duck.

I had garnered unsavoury attention. Two men were standing behind me.

I think the world's fastest runner is our brain; in nanoseconds it can roam around the whole world and come back to you.

Myriads of thoughts and scenarios flashed before my eyes. Me dead , looted ,crumpled, raped lying helplessly on a deserted highway etc etc with no one even knowing where I was, since I had been stupid and not told anyone where I was going As I was in depression, wallowing in self -pity and mostly stayed isolated, it would be a while before people noticed my absence.

Faces of all my loved ones, past and present, floated before my eyes.

Oh ! God save me! I prayed

Be strong, Be strong! I said to myself.

BE STRONG

Be strong

When you are not wrong

Don't lie tamely on the ground

To let people fuck you around

"Geeta move! Come to me You two back off Else I will shoot". I suddenly realised that the gun was pointed at them and not me.

My rooted legs now galvanised into action and I sprinted across to Sumi She who looked like a villain one moment ago, was now an angel incarnate.

Two men who looked like alcoholics/muggers thought better to back off rather than risk their head and disappeared in the dark.

We broke into a sprint and reached the dhaba. We sat down and heaved a sigh of relief And then we ordered tea, as whenever I was shaken, tea always gave me relief. I didn't feel like speaking.

My heart was still running at a break-neck speed. The first sip of tea sent a wave of relief through my body.

I had not even thanked Sumi.

I was not in a position to speak so I just reached across and clasped her hand to express my gratitude. She nodded in understanding and pressed back.

"What the hell were you thinking Geeta? That you will be able to catch the running bus on foot? Not even Usain Bolt could have caught it! Or did you think you were some Bollywood heroine? What got inside you?", she scolded me in one breath, "Do you have any idea how grave a danger you had put yourself in? Thank God I reached there on time!"

I had no words to say except listen meekly.

"Sumi! A bus seems to be approaching", I exclaimed. The headlights of the bus could be seen from a distance. The bus reached the dhaba and stopped.

And oh my goodness! We couldn't believe our eyes! It was our bus, back to pick us up!

We quickly got inside, wasting no time, boarding it quickly as if it was our life-line. The conductor had realised we weren't there and asked the driver to turn back. We thanked him and settled down in our seats

Whew! What a roller-coaster ride it had been till now and the night was not over yet. What else was in store?

I wondered what quirk of fate had made Sumi cross my path. She saved my life tonight.

It reminded me of poem I had read:

QUE SERA QUE SERA

Whatever will be will be
It is called destiny
Is everything predestined?
Is it our past life's crime?
Or some deeds committed in dark
Come out in day naked stark
I think all rolled into one
Our Karma cycle has begun

The bus was now on the highway again, piercing through the darkness of the night towards its destination.

BUS

"Like a serpent in the dark
Gliding smoothly on the path
Zigzag up and down
Moving through villages and town
Bus makes its journey ahead
Towards its goal ,in the night dead"

CHAPTER -7

Soon the hush of our return died down and everyone fell asleep.

Only we two couldn't sleep although I had closed my eyes in the semblance of sleep.

Sleep, however, was far from my eyes after all the drama that had happened. Everything kept replaying in my mind. My heart had still not relaxed.

Sumi too pretended to sleep But you can always make out if someone is sleeping or not - by the rhythm their breathing

"Who are you ? Do you always carry it ?", I asked her abruptly.

"What?"

"The gun", I said in a hushed tone.

Her eyes flew open. "I am Sumi as I have told you before No, I don't always carry it on a day-to-day basis but sometimes when I am travelling alone to unknown or lonely places, I play safe. Till now I have never had the need to use it. They back off as you saw, since no one messes with a woman who has a gun. I have learnt how to shoot and have a licensed gun for my safety".

"But why did you decide to get yourself a gun? Not everyone does that. What made you?"

Sumi smiled, "Aha! Now you want my story". She settled herself in a more restful position and tilted her pretty head " Okay! I will tell you but promise me you will also relate yours to me. By the way, who is Tarun and why did you think he had sent me to kill you?"

"Agreed !", I said, nodding my head.

Sumi started narrating her story. Her eyes were closed as if she had gone long back in time.

REMEMBERING

The river that flowed silently ado
Where I lived many moons ago
Green blue water, silvery banks
Waves and fishes playing pranks
Kingfisher ducks and egrets
All together with no regrets
Hooting owl in the night
Golden glorious morning bright
Moon shedding its light sublime
What a tranquil sight divine
Throngs of bathers of all ranges
River no other but my Holy Ganges

I could sense she was remembering some good times spent with some loved ones.

"I lived in a small town by the banks of the river Ganga

My life was beautiful, peaceful and full of joy. I had a loving, supporting family and above all Harshit.

Harshit and I were childhood friends. We were neighbours as well as schoolmates

Harshit was tall, fair and beautiful with an aquiline nose and an athletic body.

We would climb trees and play pranks together. As we grew up, I would feel jealous if Harshit talked to anyone other than me and one day we even got into a fight regarding this".

"Jealous? Why were you jealous of Sumi?" laughed Harshit.

Sumi smiled and continued, "She suddenly held me from behind and locked her arms around me. She was breathing near my ear and then gradually started kissing me on the nape of my neck Oh God! What was she doing to me? It was a new awakening for me and I was loving it.

In the heat of the moment she kissed me on my lips and it felt otherworldly Yes, Harshit was a girl. I was astonished but tHishen we both realised that we were more than just friends - we were sweethearts. I had never been so happy. I didn't know it was even possible. Even the sunshine seemed brighter and the flowers more colourful. There was a new spring to my gait.

So was the case with Harshit; she too was on cloud nine".

She paused to take a breath and began again,

"A strange energy was ensuing in us: we were like Romeo and Juliet but with a twist.

We knew what difficulties we would face. We were secretive. We turned into lovers overnight.

One day we met in an orchard. She said, "Sumu I want to marry you Until we get officially married let's exchange our tokens of love".

Do you see this locket Geeta?This was given to me by my Harshit.

I always keep it near my heart because I gave her mine. It was our secret pact. A promise of our eternal love.

People take us lightly but love is love. It is something divine to be treasured".

On hearing this I gawked at her. Sumi went on,

"She was a beautiful girl , many boys were after her but she had eyes only for me.

We wanted to live together, get married, but knew it was not easy. No, this small town wasn't going to accept our relationship. So we decided on a plan. I would look for a job in Delhi or Mumbai where people are not too nosy and later Harshit too would join me. Our plan was fool proof, at least we thought so, but to implement it we needed time.

So I started preparing hard, joined an MBA programme and moved to Delhi.

But Harshita, that was her name, I used to call her. Harshit was not so lucky. She did not have a supportive family. They did not want her to study further. She had done her graduation and that was considered enough for a girl

They were very old-school , girls were meant only for cooking, household chores and raising babies. They had educated her just so that she could fit in the marriage market.

Now they were pressing her to get married and she was becoming more and more frantic by the day. I had taken up a part-time job but time was running out on us.

She was a pretty girl and was getting lots of proposals. She had been warding them off on one pretext or the other Her family however had fixed her marriage to a rich politician's son and she was growing all berserk. Her family started growing suspicious.At first they thought she was involved with some guy but no one had ever seen her befriend a boy.They started keeping an eye on her, thinking maybe she confided in someone. I am sure there was someone who knew but I don't know who. "I will tell you later",she sounded desperate in her last call.

It was decided that she would come to Delhi. She couldn't take it anymore. I didn't know what she was tolerating since she was really closed up.

Everything was planned to great detail. She would take a bus and board a train from the nearby town in order to waylay the trail. She boarded the bus as planned and was on her way to the next city. I was really happy and waiting for her to reach Delhi.

But I waited and waited at the station and she never came. I ended up searching every coach, going mad that her phone was off.

My heart was not willing to believe what my mind was thinking.

A few days later, her body was found in the nearby fields a few kilometres from her house, brutally raped and murdered.

Someone I guess had known her plan or followed her.

On hearing about her death, I was devastated I returned to my hometown.

When I visited her house, their cold treatment said it all.

They had made a huge tamasha with her body and taken compensation in lieu of her death from the government but my heart says it was honour-killing. I didn't have any proof but the police was investigating

My Harshita, my beautiful Harshit, dead and crumpled beyond recognition".

She quoted:

THE BOOK

Her life was a book
It looked beautiful and new
Last page was bloody

"After her death I was heartbroken. I started questioning everything, every relationship. What was it between Harshita's parents and her? Was that love or hate? How can you get your child killed just for the sake of flimsy honour, just to save your ass from some hypothetical horrid scenarios? They didn't have the guts to face the world or the wrath of the politico. So they diminished her".

She started sobbing silently, pain still imminent on her face.

I hugged her tight.

LOVE HATE

Love and hate go hand in hand
They are sisters of the same band
One is dark one is light
One can harm other delight

The line between them is fine
Sometimes it just intertwines
One can't exist without other
They were born in man together
You can love or abhor some acts
This is the way we all react
We can love dogs and cats
But creep out by lizards and rats
For some hatred is driving force
Killing and torture pleasure source
Too much love also chokes
Hangs by the neck like a yoke
Extreme of both of them is bad
Lack of them too makes life bland

"So I went back to Delhi, took up a job, but a lot of anger was welling up inside me. To channelise it, I joined shooting and kick boxing on the suggestion of a friend. With time, I began to regain my calm and realised every girl should know how to protect herself. Eventually I applied for a license and got myself a gun. I have never had a cause to use it.

When I saw you running like that, I realised something bad might befall you So I came after you Thank God for that.

We LGBTQ+ people have to bear a lot. We have to fight for our simple rights and pleasures. Times are changing, more people are coming out.

We have realised that if you don't like the life you are living, don't pretend to like it but show your dislike, make efforts to change, so we are doing tha"t.

WHISPERS IN THE WIND

Love them do not hate
God's children they are
Do not berate
Bisexual lesbian gay transgender or queer
Extreme marginalisation they bear
To live with us as equals is all they ask
To give these rights , is too much a task?
Quietly they fight their own battles
Now for less they won't settle
Varied they are like rainbow
You can't just ignore and go
Coming out in open now they don't mind
Times are changing can you hear
The whispers in the wind

"I know Geeta that I will not let them go free. They will have to pay for what they did to my Harshit. I will find a way to justice sooner or later".

I looked at her determined set of expressions and I knew she would.

CHAPTER -8

Sumi was proving to be quite a surprise

Like an onion, she was revealing yet another facet of hers, after every peel.

I could never have imagined her to be queer. But how do you know about the sexual preferences of others? We have been ingrained to think only along the dotted lines that there can only be two sexes. What we don't see is permutations and combinations of God in nature. He has made variations by combinations in every form So why should we think that He will stop at just two in human sexuality? Even in sexuality He has made variations. That is where the LGBTQ+ community comes

Who are we to kill and penalise people who don't align to the dotted lines we have created? God has made everything beautiful, it's just a matter of perspective.

PERSPECTIVE

What is happiness?
Who can define
For some it is bungalows and wine
For some only a cottage is fine
Some like to dance in rain
For some it is sunshine
If you ask a monk his take
His will be devotion to divine
Some run after women and cars

For some it is moon and stars
No two persons are the same
They differ in thoughts and plane
Everything is right and sane
It is a matter of perspective
Nothing is wrong or defective
Each in its own is right
That makes the world lovely and bright
It is up to you how you look
You see good or just crooks
Your outlook shapes your life
Positive or negative you decide

I was deeply moved by her story and was thinking about how these people bear the brunt of others' lack of open-mindedness. That's why they rarely come out and reveal their true identity, I thought, especially women who are forced into loveless marriages. They hide their true identity and happiness in a closet

Sumi pressed my hand. "Thank you", she said, "I needed that. I had been bottling all this up for so long. It feels good now. I am feeling lighter, as if a load has been lifted.

How strange we humans are, we hide our anguish from our loved ones but bare our souls to strangers, I guess because we are afraid of being judged Their opinions matter to us but it is not so with strangers. That's where counsellors and psychiatrists come into play. They are strangers but listen to us empathetically and do not judge us for our deeds. I think that must have been the idea behind confession rooms in churches It must have helped the mental state of many".

JUDGING

Never judge anyone by his strides
You never know what he hides
From how far he has come
Had he been hurt or welcomed
His shoes are worn or new
Will hint at miles more or few
You know not what he has been through
Unless you slip into his shoes
On which foot the shoe bites
Before judging anyone think twice
Did he have any other choice
Why someone acted in particular way
How many options he had his way
If we had been in the same situation
Had we taken the same options
Choices and situations change with time
Too easy to judge others for their crime
Every coin has two sides
Look at both before you decide

I looked outside the window, it was pitch black. The bus was running on a completely dark road with its headlights paving the way. Have you ever seen a snake gliding across water smoothly and swiftly making its way ? Yes! The bus reminded me of that. It was a little while before dawn.
I took a sip of water and said, "From where should I start?"
"From the beginning they say it is a good idea", said Sumi.

Geeta started speaking slowly, her face sombre.

THE LEAF

I was a new leaf
Soft and green
Giddy with beauty and sheen
At the top carefree
How away was I,
From my roots
Attached to the tree
Strong winds jostled me around
But I stuck my ground
Autumn come
I started to change
Green to beautiful yellow red
I fell down dead
Crushed mercilessly by boots
I was now beside my roots

CHAPTER-9

Tarun and I met at a common friend's house. He was tall, dark, handsome and a total charmer. I was 24 years old and naïve. He swept me off my feet. He would bring me flowers and gifts, open doors and pull out chairs. I was bowled over.

He proposed to me and I accepted!

My parents were not happy with him. They asked me to wait, asked me how much I knew about him but I was blind in his love.

He worked in a multi-national company but my father was a wise man, he asked me to look at his career-chart; he had not worked for long in any job.

"He doesn't seem to be a steady person", my father said. He also asked me to look at his family background. His father was a womaniser. "An apple doesn't fall far from its tree", he had said wisely but I was not ready to listen to any of the reasons.

We got married. I was happy and felt like a queen. He was the most attentive in the initial days. However, I did not know that this queen's tiara I had adorned was full of thorns.

Gradually the novelty started wearing off. He sweetly coaxed me into getting a job. He could be the most persuasive and sweetest when he wanted something, this I had learned the hard way

I took up a job and started working. He would often come back home grumbling about office issues One day he did the unthinkable - he slapped his boss and was chucked out. I came to know this later. He told me he had resigned ,he couldn't work under someone and would start his own business. Now I was the breadwinner and I was the cook and maid-in-hand, as you rightly said in that poem He would wait for my pay cheques and take control of them. "The arrogant bastard ","Thinks too highly of himself", I thought, but never voiced my opinions

He would say that I was not good at finances so he would take care of my money.

I was earning but I was not in control of my money.

When I became pregnant I thought things would change but this was not in his plans. He started degrading me by calling me ugly, hitting me, bruising me. One time he would be a monster and at other times he would apologise and be loving and sweet.

I was caught in a vicious cycle. Which one was his true self? But we should know that both the sides were his sides as no one is totally dark all the time. Everyone has shades of grey, but how deep and how grey the person is, that matters.

The Tarun I knew before marriage and after were completely different personalities. Then he had only shown his one side. But that is how it is, you can meet people for months with a mask on, if you meet them for a short while. But living with them is an entirely different matter.

Then the mask wears off. You might be best friends for years but you might not necessarily be a good living-partner or mate. I had overlooked red flags which my father had been warning me about.

He would stay at home. Nit-picking my work. I used to feel glad about my job, at least it took me away from him. Many years passed this way.

He would beat me and then make love. He said beating turned him on. When women were going gaga over that book 'Fifty Shades of Grey', I hated it. I thought how foolish they were. Don't even touch such a man with a barge-pole! I was living the nightmare. Reading and hearing about it doesn't seem so severe. You might even fancy it in your dreams But living it is a nightmare.

DOMESTIC VIOLENCE

***D**onning makeup*
***O**ver the*
***M**arks of hurts*
***E**very time*
***S**miling in front of others*
***T**o not let others know,what*
***I**nside they bear at home,women*
***C**ry silently, caught in the*
***V**icious cycle of beating & treating*
***I**n the very hands*
***O**f their*
***L**oved ones, who act like their*
***E**nemies*
***N**eglected, Abused, Degraded*
***C**onfidence lost, this must*
***E**nd at all costs.*

STOP DOMESTIC VIOLENCE

I felt hesitant to talk about my ordeal to my parents as I had gone against their wishes to marry him. I had lost all confidence and felt ashamed to reveal what I was going through.

Besides, they were not getting any younger. My pain would have hurt them immensely. I loved them greatly.

He knew my raw spots and made full use of it. One of my friends told me that Tarun was seeing someone on the sly. At first I couldn't believe it. So I started looking for proof and I easily found it in his chat box.

He never had a habit of locking his phone. I was not the snoopy type, never ever cared to snoop around his things. How trusting, stupid and naive I was.

It was a jolt from the blue. The sane advice of my father came rushing into my mind; he indeed was proving to be his father's son.

As they say, kids learn by the examples their parents set ,not their admonitions. So he had. For the first time I was angry with him, with myself and with this world. Whatever it was, all pent-up frustration or pregnancy hormones, I confronted him immediately. He denied it outright. When faced with proof he became violent but this time I was not backing down. I too fought tooth and nail. He was taken by surprise by this newfound energy of mine. He pushed me hard and I fell down flat on the ground and next thing I knew, everything was black.

When I woke up, I was in the hospital. I had lost my baby. Tarun was sitting beside me - epitome of sweetness, kindness and a doting husband.

But I knew better. It was all facades. He had two personalities like Jekyll and Hyde.

After the loss of my baby something died inside me. It felt like I was watching everything from an outsider's point of view, whatever was happening was happening to someone else.

I had become numb. Was I living life mechanically like a zombie?

Even Tarun sensed that. He said, "Don't worry Geeta, we will have another baby. You just get well soon".

Men are so heartless; as if it doesn't matter I will buy you another toy. Was it all to him? It was a little life inside me anticipating to come out...

MISCARRIAGE

You came into the womb of mine
My baby, I was on cloud nine
Every day on fingers will count
When you will on my lap mount
Daily to you I would talk
Your every moment I would stalk
One night I woke up with intense pain
I knew my fears were not in vain
I was bleeding from my womb
My womb had become your tomb
I couldn't save you how much I tried
My poor baby, my poor child
I cried, cried, cried, and cried

More than physical my soul was hurt
Did I do something, was it my mistake?
The life of my baby which it take
I was floundering in my grief
A boat in shoreless ocean deep
I felt alone numb and mute
I guess I needed a loving lute
It is traumatic to lose an unborn life
To overcome this takes a while
Love and family support they need
Their health too they should heed

When my parents heard about my miscarriage, they came rushing to meet me.

Tarun was the epitome of grace. Only I had become numb. His sweeter than saccharin attitude made me nauseous.

I showed no emotions, neither happiness nor pain, at seeing them. I felt vacant. They thought I had taken the loss of the baby too much to heart but actually it was an amalgamation of everything.

My parents suggested to Tarun that I was probably in depression and a change of scenery would do me good. So I should come with them to stay for a few days. Now Tarun was trapped by playing doting husband, he had to agree reluctantly. I knew he was watching my every reaction and every move. I remained silent and passive.

I packed my things in a small case. He even had the audacity to check what I was taking! I didn't object to his intrusion. I felt nothing. But he was still suspicious.

"Geeta don't try to trick me. Thinking you could run away from me. I would trace you wherever you are and kill you then and there", he said menacingly, "I am just warning you".

Still getting no response from me, he let it go as he had already said what he wanted, to me.

He too was scared I guess, his meal ticket might be slipping away from his hands.

I had hidden my certificates and papers in my parents' luggage. I knew he would check my luggage again. So he did.

After finding nothing worthy inside, satisfied, he let me go. As the train left the station I could not believe it. I was leaving that godforsaken place I had called home. They say whatever happens, happens for good. I got released from the clutches of that monster but at what cost.

'Freedom' after sacrificing my poor baby. My baby had made the supreme sacrifice for its mother. My heart ached for my unborn baby.

But, was I free from the monster?

CHAPTER -10

I reached my parents' house. It felt strange. They had preserved my room as I had left it. They were doting more, caring more than ever before. I felt crass. At this age I should be the one taking care of them not the other way around.

"I am so sorry I have troubled you mom. I am not a good daughter. I am a pain around the neck", I said tears rolling down my cheeks.

"No no my child, why do you think so? You are the best daughter anyone can have. It can happen to anyone, don't blame yourself. My poor baby", my mother hugged me for a long time.

A mother's hug is always consoling. You feel a sense of security and coming home.

After a few days, the nightmares started. I would wake up screaming, wet with perspiration. My parents would rush to my side. I would have difficulty sleeping. Then my bouts of crying started. Now my parents were really concerned. I did not feel like eating. I was sinking into depression.

DEPRESSION

When you have trouble sleeping
Feel like endlessly weeping
Life doesn't seem fair
Waking up seems a nightmare
You feel hollow from inside

Lonely although friends beside
Your heart races at breakneck speed
You don't feel the need to feed
Don't just let it go
It is depression you know
Please seek help
Go to a doc
You will come out of this lock
It is nothing to be ashamed
You are not to be blamed
It is a health issue like other
Meant to be treated like any other

My parents were astute. They were worldly wise. They understood there was more to it than what meets the eye. We underestimate our parents, thinking we are wiser and more intelligent than them. But we forget they have travelled these paths before us and faced similar situations before. They know our every nuance and can read our unspoken miseries.

They understood I would not be revealing anything to them so they took me to a counsellor.

I was a nervous wreck. I had a complete mental breakdown.

Tarun played caring husband and would often phone to enquire about me and when I would be back.

He knew I was no use to him in this condition. I was better off at my parents'. So he did not object much.

I told the counsellor I was having nightmares. I would often dream I am running and running then falling in a deep dark pit. I would scream for help. And wake up. The most recurring nightmare was the one where I am running on a pitch dark road, running and running at top speed, always waking up with the vision of a gun pointed towards me.

Do you know Sumi? When I saw you with a gun on that dark road, I had a sense of deja vu It was my worst nightmare coming true but I had not imagined it to be this way. I think we were destined to meet.

These psychiatrists are very smart people they guess quite a lot from your body language, dreams etc.

She straightaway asked me how my married life was. I was reluctant at first then I gradually opened up in the next sessions. I later related everything to my parents too in bits. Your life's misery is such, you can only tell in short phases when the memory surfaces.

They were angry with me for not telling them anything and bearing so much. My father would go into bouts of angry litany. The very thought of someone raising their hand on women, above all his precious daughter, was abhorrent to him.

But they decided to go wisely about it. He would say, "Don't act crazy with a crazy man. Find a saner way out". They advised me to not go back to him. But I was worried about my safety and theirs".

The numbness in my heart and the fogginess in my brain was slowly going away. But I was not my old self. I think you can never be your old self, your self changes every day with time and experience. Life had taught me some bitter lessons in a short span of time. Can I unlearn those lessons? No, no one can unless you have amnesia.

I had lost confidence in myself. I had started believing all those ugly things which Tarun had been saying to me.

I had trouble relating to people. I must have done some good deeds in my past life to get such a loving, caring and supportive pair of parents.

Physically I was okay but mentally every day was a battle. I had to instruct myself regularly to get up from bed and go about my daily business.

The thought of my parents kept me going, their worried faces and their efforts to make everything seem normal for me, urged me on.

On my counsellor's advice I started writing a journal, putting down all my bottled up feelings. I would jot down all good and bad incidents, my thoughts and perceptions. This helped me a great deal.

I was advised to dress up nice, look into the mirror everyday and say to myself, 'I am beautiful, smart intelligent and brave and can achieve anything'.

To me first it seemed liked a stupid idea but gradually, I started feeling good from inside. The nightmares also started receding.

I realised that the key to everything is loving ourselves the way we are".

LOVE YOURSELF

God has created
everyone beautiful
Ugly is the view
of the beholder

Who knows not
How to create
But can only
Annihilate
God created us
In his image
But we criticise
The very visage
Beauty lies in variation
It is a cause of celebration
Black, white pale brown
Fat thin up down
Tall short fat or thin
We should be happy
From within
Love your life,
love your body
Confidently move
with everybody
Don't changc it for anybody's likes
Your body your style
This advice helped me a ton.

CHAPTER -11

"My parents advised me to take up a job once more and file for divorce - if I was ready for it. It was easier said than done. I had lost all confidence. I had to start all over again. The fear of his threat always loomed large over me. I was again taking the baby steps.

Tarun's calls for my return were increasing. I was avoiding him. Then I took the bravest step. Although I was fearful and quivering from inside, I decided to stand up against the monster.

I sent him a divorce letter through my lawyer. He came like a raging bull. But I was unfazed. He tried to be sweet as well as angry , but it was of no use now. Then he came in his full menacing form. Hissing like an angry snake. Spitting venom. But he could not control and hit me here, besides we had installed CCTV cameras. Sometimes we paralyse ourselves with over analyzing. Taking no decisions is the worst decision. This, I was learning with time.

Now was the next step. I had to seek a job and I got myself one. It really helped me. I started getting my confidence back. But agony cannot be expressed in words. What I had endured with him can't be related like a tale. Years of physical abuse and mental torture leaves an indelible mark".

HEALING

When do you know you have healed?
When it stops to pain?
Or
When the scar is gone?

"My progress was at a snail's pace. It was very slow. I had trust issues. I still have. But I made progress.

I changed jobs and places. But that threat of Tarun still niggled somewhere at the back of my mind. I know him quite well. He is the Devil in disguise. He will come for me.

That's why I thought he had sent you to kill me. I had been living the same routine life for a long time, like a mechanical robot going to the office and back.

Life had become quite dull. Several people advised me to take a hiatus from work. So finally I am out on vacation".

I looked out from the window. The sun was rising. We had reached Himachal. The sight was rejuvenating.

MORNING

Beautiful sun rises from its bed
Spreading its tentacles red
Sky welcomes with open arms
Mountains basking in its warmth
When the sun on flowers loom
Lotus in their ponds bloom
It engulfs the darkest night
Washes earth silvery bright

It looks around at misty hue
On the trembling pearly dew
Elves and goblins of the night
Now disappear out of sight
What a beauty nature weaves
When sun winks through the leaves

The bus was travelling on beautiful mountainous roads. The night had ended and the sun had risen like the harbinger of a new beginning. How symbolic. We both had spent our journey and night in retrospection. We had embarked on this bus as strangers but had shared our woes as long lost friends. Strange are the ways of life; we will be parting again at the next stop perhaps never to meet again but one thing I am sure of. I will remember her and this journey all my life. The bus reached McLeodganj. Sumi and I parted ways. She gave me her number But 'old habits die hard'; I didn't give her mine. Yes , I still couldn't trust her fully. After all, she was just a stranger. How much did I know about her really? She understood and nodded that it was okay and I could call her if I needed her. This beautiful gesture of hers made me respect her more. I wished her happiness and we parted ways. Fluglar Hostel was my next destination.

Sumi took a cab and reached her hotel 'Royal'. It was a beautiful place situated in scenic surroundings.

Actually the whole of McLeodganj was beautiful. Wherever she turned her head she encountered beauty.

Her room was quite good as well overlooking a green valley She had changed into pyjamas and was at ease now, having ordered sandwiches and tea. She would soon be relaxing with her cup beside her window seat.

Thoughts of last night's incidents and Geeta came unheeded to her mind. She became sombre. There was something in her that had gravitated her towards her to talk. As if they were destined to meet. It was an unusual journey. She had a gut feeling that Geeta would contact her sooner or later. But for now she needed to call someone and apprise of last night's events.

She got up from her seat to fetch her phone which was on the bed side table and started dialling. The bell kept on ringing. No one answered. She tried calling again. Same result. Maybe I will try later, she thought.

Chapter 12

The hostel was on a cliff. You had to trek up to reach the hostel. I mentally thanked my counsellor who had advised me to do yoga and other physical activities for my anxiety and depression. It had helped a great deal in elevating my moods as well as my physical health. I could easily climb with my backpack. The hostel was a little away from the main city Quite picturesque and peaceful.

It was such a beautiful place, so colourful with a homely ambience. Colourful graffiti Impeccable lawns and flowers Such positive vibes it exuded.

Surrounded by mountains , the fresh air here hit so different from Delhi's air I took a deep breath. Yes this was something I had been missing in my life Peace.

My room was clean and colourful, inviting with a very beautiful view.

Last night had been quite eventful. I informed my parents of my whereabouts before they started worrying. They had been pillars of support in my testing times.

I showered and ordered tea and sandwiches. The tea was good and the sandwiches felt delicious to my hungry, rumbling stomach. Maybe I felt a bit relaxed and the scenery was good, so I was already feeling better. Let me lie down for a while, I decided, then I will have a look around. As soon as my head hit the pillow I reached sleep-land. I had not realised how tired I was, both mentally and physically I woke up to a dark room and switched on the bedside lamp. I had been sleeping the whole day. The night sky sprinkled with stars was visible from my window.

It was only eight o' clock. Nights descend early in the mountains. In Delhi it is just evening at this time and people work till late night. I was feeling fresh. I checked myself in the mirror and put some gloss on my lips. It added a little colour to my otherwise pale face. I was ready to explore this new place. I went down to the family room or what you call a common room It was a great place.

To me it seemed like an artist's heaven. You could sing, play, write, muse, read or just laze around. People were sitting there, chilling and doing their own things. You must have gathered by now that my mind had a habit of meandering into poetic by-lanes, at the most unusual of times and places. I guess poets are different, they can get inspiration from the most unusual objects and this place was sitting in the lap of beauty. My attention got attracted towards a gentleman. He was tall, around 6 feet, athletic-built with very short hair, handsome in a rugged sort of way. I recognised him as the same guy from my bus. He introduced himself as Frank He was an ex - serviceman and now ran a security providing agency. He provided security, bodyguards etc to stars and the rich.

He was a poet as well and an animal-lover too. People say animal-lovers are good at heart but you may never know, I thought sceptically. "Oh ! You are the same person who was left in Karnal". He recognised me immediately. "Yes", I said blushing, feeling embarrassed about what a fiasco that had been. "Geeta", I introduced myself. "It is a beautiful place", I said I was a lousy talker who didn't know how to initiate a conversation

"Yeah!", he smiled , a smile that reached up to his eyes making him look attractive.

"I come here often enough whenever I get time. This place soothes my mind and body Enough material for me to write". He said.

"What do you write?", I asked.

"Poems, fiction, columns, whatever fancies me".

"I think here we both have something in common, I write as well", came out of my mouth. "Really ! That's good, that makes two of us then. It will be good, we will both share our attempts at being a bard". We both broke into laughter. It felt good. "Tomorrow is camping and a bonfire. Would you like to go with us?", he added.

"Would love to", I nodded in the affirmative. It had been a long time since I had had such an experience. I was excited.

Once I had done so in my college days Now it seemed like a lifetime ago. I had been living in a shell for too long now and I wanted to start living again, experience the sun and the rain once again. This thought was a pleasant change. I guess this place was weaving its magic. My heart wanted to throw all caution to the wind, it just wanted to be free and enjoy the present. I just didn't want to think about anything depressing. I went up to my room after having a delicious dinner. My appetite seemed to be picking up. Maybe it was a change of scenery or the trek I had done to reach here It had been good till now. Tomorrow would be another day.

TOMORROW IS ANOTHER DAY

What you have is the present time
Make hay when the sun shines
Past is gone gone for good
You know not what the future holds
It is trash or is it gold
Keep your fingers crossed
For best you pray, enjoy now
Tomorrow is another day

I relived all the happenings of the day. I changed into my pyjamas, brushed my teeth and combed my hair. Then I looked into the mirror. Was it my imagination or was there a little spark of anticipation in my eyes? It had been long since I had looked forward to waking up in the morning.

I think mountain air was doing me good. I slept soundly and woke up to the beautiful view of the rising sun from my window. Some visitors were out, enjoying the scenery. I got out of my bed, a new spring to my feet, went ahead quickly with my morning routine of pooping and brushing. And then, out I was clad in my jogging suit

I did not want to miss out on a beautiful morning. Every moment here was precious to me. Cool, fresh air was blowing against my body. My poetic heart was playing its own symphony.

DANCE OF NATURE

Fresh air in my hair
Blows away despair
Plays with trees and plants

Makes them sway and slant
Nature's beautiful dance
Puts me in trance
Butterfly flowers trees
Ants spiders and bees
Cooing doves soaring hawks
Incredible! You just gawk

"Aha! here you are. I didn't know you were a morning person". Frank's voice brought me out from my reverie. "Am I intruding on your poetic thoughts?", he asked politely. "No ! No "! I lied, "I was just admiring the scenery". "Is that it ? If you say so. You seemed so engrossed, I was watching you and have been standing here for long. So I thought maybe you have found your muse". "I didn't hear you approach", I replied. "Yeah I had guessed that". It was so easy to engage in conversation with him, I didn't at all feel threatened. Our conversation easily drifted from one topic to another.

"Have you had your breakfast?", he asked. I nodded in denial

"Let's go and have it now. We walked together to the open area to have our breakfast on a beautiful sunny morning in the mountains". I ordered Aloo Paratha and tea. He was having an omelette and toast with coffee. We both were sitting quietly and enjoying our food and moments of peace. 'Far from the madding crowd.'

Frank sat in his room reflecting on the day's events.

After so many years , he had felt a stirring in his heart. He had been inadvertently drawn towards the girl with the dark eyes that spoke. There was an aura of vulnerability about her. It brought out a protective instinct inside him.

She intrigued him. What ailed her, what made her tick- he wanted to find out all Her smile would light up her face but it never reached her eyes hinting at deep hurt and loneliness. She had camouflaged it well. Deep sadness in her eyes had hit a chord. When she was lost in thoughts and musing, her pink lips trembled. That beauty spot on her lips increased her sensuality. He had a feeling she had caged herself behind a wall. He wanted to crack that open and know the real Geeta. He was surprised at the direction his thoughts were taking. "God am I going crazy?", he muttered to himself. Her poetic disposition had surprised him. They both had some common interests. After Sheena had gone from his life, he had lost faith in happiness. Geeta's company, though for a short span, had a soothing effect. He was looking forward to her company tomorrow. Did this mean his frozen heart was thawing at last? He switched on the television and started flicking the channels. Most were showing old Hindi movies He flicked the channel to one with a wildlife series going on. Nature had always held a special attraction to him. Hiking. travelling and writing were his hobbies. His stint in the army had made him take physical fitness seriously. At four and forty years young, he could easily be taken as five years younger. He was sporty and met people, but loneliness had started gnawing at him. He watched the sun rising from the sea, the dolphins saluting the golden orb. After watching for a while he switched off the television. He let out a big yawn and went off to sleep.

Before closing his eyes, his last thoughts were of her big, dark eyes.

EYES

Eyes are mirror to one's soul
Senora! Those angelic eyes of yours
Hold me in their allure
What a magic they weave
Dark like ocean deep
They beckon me even in sleep
Oh! Senora, who are you?
I know not ,when our eyes meet
My heart skips a beat

Chapter 13

We decided to sit on the grass, each lost in their own world. It was pleasant, sunny and warm. I was observing the antics of a lizard and a fluttering butterfly Wherever I looked, I found poetry. No wonder so many writers and poets made their abodes in hill stations. I started musing aloud.

LIZARD AND THE BUTTERFLY

Says Lizard to the butterfly
Fly as much you high
Little one! Your end is nigh
I will catch you
How much you fly
Lizard made few tries
Just a futile exercise
You go your way O!Lizard sly
I will fly away to the sky
Said the pretty butterfly
Freedom doesn't come easy by
I have struggled hard and dry
Several stages I passed by
Was locked in a cocoon dry
Its dark walls I had to pry
Then I found my wings to fly
Will not let it go easily by
She flitted away in the sky
Lizard turned its face wry
Paid attention to unwary fly

Who was sitting nearby
Slurp! Chomp! In went the fly
Victory to the Lizard sly
No butterfly so what!
There are other fishes to fry

"Good ! Very good ! a poetess in action. Yeah you observe well". I had forgotten Frank was sitting near me and listening to me compose aloud. "Oh ! They are okayish. I just write what I feel". "Isn't that what we all do?", Frank said and added, "but rhythm and sensitivity make a poem and decide how deep it touches you". "Yeah", I nodded in agreement. "Would you like to play some board game? There are some kept there". He went ahead and brought a Scrabble. "All others were taken, I could find just this".

In reply I said, "It is as good as any, let's play for a while". He was a good player with a good vocab "Are you married?"

The sudden question made me look up into his eyes. "Once I was, not anymore", I replied. "I am a divorcee. What about you?" "I too am single. My lovely wife left me for heaven. I am a widower. She died of complications at childbirth".

" Oh ! I am so sorry to hear that", I said, " What about kids?"

"No, I don't have any. The baby also did not survive", he paused and continued, "Sheena was the love of my life. I did not feel like getting married again. My mother started living with me. I had lost my father at a young age. She had been a single mother but she too left me alone to join Sheena in heaven soon after. My siblings are busy with their lives and families. I live alone. I had taken VRS to take care of my ailing mother, she

had become like a child in her last days. Alzheimer's had taken her over. My sane, intelligent mother would play like a child and became totally dependent on me and then one night she passed away peacefully into another world. I started my own security agency and immersed myself in work. Have you heard about the poetess Annie? She was my mother". "Annie !" I exclaimed, "she used to write beautifully". "She passed on that gift to me. I too indulge in poems and writing as I have told you before". I could sense his pain. No one in this world is happy although they may appear so. Each has to bear their own cross. He got up, "Let's go now. I would advise you to take some rest after lunch as camping and trekking are almost a whole night affair and quite strenuous". We gathered the Scrabble pieces together and headed towards the common room. He returned the Scrabble to its place and we went to our respective rooms. I showered and rested for a while, got dressed and went down again. After all, I had not come here to sit in my room. I asked the receptionist about what all was there to see around so I could plan my day and the rest of the time of my stay here. I asked them,"what time would they be camping"?

"In the evening, around 6 o'clock", they said to me. "I can take a taxi and look around the market and local handicrafts. I'll come back again on time for the trip", I said. "Ma'am don't miss this camping trip! It is not organised on a regular basis. We do that only when enough people are there and the climate is good", the man at the reception informed. I took an Ola and went down to see the market. There were beautiful handicraft shops. I decided to buy a cap for my father and a shawl for my mother, some souvenirs and some magnetic stickers to adorn my refrigerator. My refrigerator had a lot of souvenirs from all the places I had visited. The lady of the emporium asked me to sign

the visitor book with my phone number and what I thought of her products. I obliged and gave her raving reviews. There was another lady in a traditional dress, sitting on a stool in the shadows. She seemed familiar. I had a feeling I had seen her before but could not place where. I thought maybe she resembles someone I know or someone on TV. I went around the market absorbing all the beautiful colours and the energy and then headed back to my hostel. Good I was back on time, an hour or so before the camping trip began Except for that Karnal incident , this trip was proving to be great.

Was it really though? A thought niggled at the back of my mind. I brushed it aside. I wouldn't let my anxiety take over me and my attempts at happiness.

CHAPTER-14

All who wished to join in the camping trip had gathered in the common area The guide was giving instructions about dos and don'ts. Stick together. Don't wander alone into the woods. It is very easy to get lost in the jungle, all trees look the same. No throwing trash around. Wear shoes and covering clothes. No tigers here but other wildlife exists. So be careful of snakes,scorpions etc. No smoking in the jungle. We were all to carry our water bottles with us always , leader's number and location, etc. We all noted these in our mobiles. How easier our life has become with mobiles. But we are becoming too dependent on it too. When we start relying on it too much we stop listening to our other senses. We don't look, feel, absorb or analyse ourselves. We just find the quickest way out and let mobiles do the thinking for us. Aren't we becoming too lazy, not even wanting to tax our brains? Our ancestors achieved so much without any aids. I was lost in my thoughts.

"Shall we proceed Ms, if you are ready ?", Frank's voice brought me out from my reverie. "Yeah sure! I am". We all started our trek in groups of fours and fives and were full of energy. I had taken a small bag with water and some snacks. The memory of Sumi came unhindered out of the blue "I always am prepared ". I smiled thinking about her. The trek was beautiful, we were climbing up and up, our path lined by bushes and trees We even crossed a rivulet of water. The sun had started painting the sky in myriads of colours. Shadows had started to descend on the trees. The crimson purple sky forming the backdrop of the mountains and trees left me thunderstruck. I

stopped to stare and capture the precious ever-changing moments of nature. I hadn't realised Frank had moved close to me. I could feel his body heat. He too was entranced by the amazing sight. We both were perched on a rock. I could feel his breath on my hair and it was giving me goosebumps. I tried to move away and slipped a bit but his hand shot out and steadied me. "Be careful !" I felt a jolt of electricity pass. He was lost in his own world and was softly muttering under his breath.

AMAZING NATURE

Isn't it
See glorious sun rising from the sea
How majestic it can be
See it setting in the west
In its splendour going to rest
Lie on the ground in night and wait
See moon sailing with graceful gait
Among twinkling stars eyes
Just tune your heart and ears along
You will hear night singing its song
Lovelorn 'CHAKOR' around the moon
Gazing at her lover in swoon
Chorus of crickets and owl's hoot
May give your adrenaline a boost
Air rippling through the trees
Feel the pleasant morning breeze
See the birds and fishes in morning glory
Narrating creators beautiful story
Amazing nature at its best
Just sit, smell, see and take some rest

"Beautiful!", I said.

"Not as beautiful as you Senorita!"

It was a magical moment that lasted a minute but filled me with warmth. My cold heart started its own tempo and I quickly moved ahead. It had been a long time since someone had called me beautiful. I was afraid lest he hear it. We kept on walking oblivious to others

"Senorita, move a little faster or we will be left behind". I increased my pace.

We finally reached our campsite. It was a plain patch of land. A bonfire was already burning ,some benches and tables made of logs were there. A barbecue had also been arranged Appetising smells were surrounding the area. It seemed like it was quite a regular camping area. Small tents were pitched around and the area was oozing positive vibes. Everyone got energised just by looking at it. We all took our seats on the benches and were offered welcome drinks. Now we were all relaxing around the bonfire, snacking in between, choosing from a plethora of starters. A young man started playing his guitar and singing. Once his song ended, another started singing, then someone cracked a joke in between and then one of the girls started playing songs on her phone. Everyone fell into a jig I was enjoying myself. "Let's dance?", Frank asked me softly.

"I don't know how to", I replied blushing. "I have two left feet".

"It doesn't matter. Do you think everyone here has been trained? Just let your hair down and move with the rhythm" I reluctantly got up and entered the circle. Soon I was enjoying myself and was doing pretty okay. Long lost Geeta was now coming out from the hiding.

We were all tired and the buffet was ready. An assortment of dishes and drinks.were served The money we had deposited was worth the experience. After having our fill, we became more relaxed "Look", Frank said, "Stars here seem brighter and more beautiful. Can you see The Great Bear?" "Yeah! it's enchanting". "Reminds me of Luceafărul by Mihai Emnescu" I added. "Have you read that too?", Frank asked. The night was casting its spell on us. It was proving to be quite different from what I had imagined. I was getting drawn towards Frank. My mind was warning me:

Beware! Haven't you travelled this path before? But the heart has its own reasons. My heart was saying in protest that this was only momentary and we both would be going on our separate ways soon, perhaps never to meet again. So why not enjoy the present?

We were sitting a little away from the group and talking. The group called us as they had again gathered around the bonfire to start story-narration and anecdotes. We were all in a high mood. The full moon night was increasing the romance. I started telling a tale,

LEGEND OF THE WEREWOLF

I will narrate you a tale
Of love and curse
In my way of
Rhythm and verse
Once the beautiful valley of Doon
Was ravaged by notorious goons
They looted and killed
Whoever they willed

There lived in the valley a lovely lass
Intelligent brave full of class
Moved by the valley 's plight
Decided to learn sword fight
To learn all tricks of the blade
She hired a young man called Glade
They would practice
On mountains and jungles
Their hearts too
Started to mingle
Oblivious to one observer
They became lovers
He was that nefarious goon
Who terrorised the valley of Doon
He had eyed the lovely girl
In jealousy his toes curled
With rage he was filled
Decided to get Glade killed
When lovers will meet
By the stream
He will kidnap the girl
Of his dreams
With the girl away
He would ride
Will throw Glade 's body
In the wild
As per his plan he stood
He waylaid them in the woods
Goon was in for a surprise
He couldn't get easily his prize
They both started to fight

It was a full moon night
Goons were many
They were two
For them it was die or do
Star crossed lovers tried their best
Many goons they laid to rest
They fought till their last breath
The lady cursed him before death
Oh! By this lovers moon
I curse you O! Nefarious goon
You will never to anyone belong
Whenever the moon will sing its song
You will also howl along
Today's night will always hound
You will be neither man nor hound
People say he is still around
Centuries passed but roams the ground
So they say when the moon is full
It is the night of the werewolf

Wow ! Everyone started to clap. What a story and what a splendid way of narration!

Now it was Frank's turn.

We were all looking at him expectantly.

CHAPTER-15

"My story is not so dramatic and as interesting as Geeta's. Can I take the liberty of calling you by your first name?" he asked me.

"Sure sure", I replied.

"I will tell you a simple story which sounds ordinary to the ear but was not so in real life."

THE WARRIOR QUEEN

There lived a warrior queen
Amongst us in between
She came as a bride in her teens
To unknown house world unseen
To meet her slightly elder groom
Radiant beautiful flower in bloom
They both started a journey of love
And were happy as a pair of dove
They were happy and content
Accepting whatever life sent
Oh! How the happy times ride
They had four kids by their side

Suddenly their life turned downhill
Husband one day fell down ill
Wife called doctors far and wide
Tended him never leaving his side
It was fate or evil eye

Her beloved husband died
The bride became a young widow
With four little children in tow
She longed for her lover, for him she cried
But he won't come back, how much she tried
As if she had fallen in abyss dark
No glimmer of hope or spark
Even against all odds
She always bowed to the Lord
Always praying for his mercy divine
Oh! God help me if I sinned against thine
After crying day and night
She woke up from her plight
Decided to do what was right
Put up a fight for her kids rights

They needed her most in their lives
She had to rear them and survive
Like tigress with cubs in woods
She protected them as she could
Many hardships she did face
Brought them up with grit and grace

Tough times don't last but tough people do
She was an example for me and you
When she thought her children were earning, settled and hitched
Fate showed her, it is a mean little bitch
Like king and queens story we have known
She was ditched by son of her own
When She was happy playing granny

Her youngest son turned to villainy
He threw her out of the house
With harshest words like a louse
She with elder son moved to new place
Here she lived peacefully with grace
Life now was happy and calm
After miseries like a balm
But her son had broken her heart
She would cry often, wake up with a start

Neither she abused nor curse utter
Like a true good pious mother
How can I curse a child of mine
For whom I have prayed to God divine
She was an honest woman of piety
Always helping poor and needy
She warred with hurdles all her life
Like a queen conquering in her stride
As she proceeded to old age
Her memory started to fade
Alzheimer's took over her mind
Leaving her like a child behind
One day God called her to his side
Finished was her fight against the tide
Now she peacefully in grave resides
Her beloved husband by her side

Everyone applauded his story too. I knew he was actually relating the story of his mother. His ode to her. My hand went out on its own will and covered his hand to show my understanding.

He too covered mine with his. The warmth of his hand warmed me from inside.

I was feeling like a giddy teenager. What was happening to me?

The wall which I had built around my heart was developing cracks.

Light and heat from outside had started to enter it. My icy heart was gradually thawing. A strange happiness filled my body.

Now it was another boy's turn to tell a story.

MIRROR

Once in the land of yore
Quite a long time before
There lived a king
He had a magic mirror
Every question it would answer
Guess it was like google of today
Having every answer in its array
What they didn't know it was science pure
Perpetuated as magic just to lure
Everyone believed what it said
But it said only what was fed
Mirror 's every advice king would heed
"Mirror mirror on the wall " was the password to proceed
It would advise king if he should be fighting
Or he should proceed to go in hiding
King started losing his will to think
Gradually started becoming a wimp
Mirror was a mole planted by the enemy group
Enemy then marched with his troops

He knew the king was addicted to mirror
Without its advice would move hither and thither

He had control over king 's mind
Victory was not far behind
King realised his mistake quite late
When the army was upon his gate
He lamented before being slain
Why did I rely on someone else's brain?

"Beautiful Apoorva!" ; that was the boy's name He got a lot of accolades from everyone.
Another girl was next.

FAVOURITISM

Mirror mirror on the wall
Who is the favourite of us all
Is it the person nearest to you
Or watching from the side
Or standing at a distance
It's up to you to decide
Do mirrors tell the truth
Or do they often lie
Do they have their own agenda
When they decide
Is everyone equal in their eyes?
But mirror had short sight
He didn't like the child who was forthright
He chose the nearest one whom he could control
This favouritism by the mirror took its toll
Child in the side knew not where he stood

If he was bad or was he good
They grew up with different issues
One had a big ego
The other just let it go
While the third hated mirrors
Never paying heed
"Favouritism in children grave injustice indeed "
"Awesome!" Everyone clapped.

Some of the girls had started feeling tired and wanted to return to the hostel while some were willing to stay back

Now it was a strange situation, so Frank offered to lead the girls to the hostel and whoever wanted to come along. I too decided to accompany him as the thought of his company and my cosy hostel bed was more appealing.

We all were walking in a casual pace The scenery which had looked beautiful during the day now looked dark and menacing with trees casting their shadows in haphazard forms

When you are in a jungle your primitive instincts are revived and you become alert to every sound. Although night is the time to rest, the jungle never sleeps.

After walking for about an hour we reached a spot where a van had been arranged for us to take us back to the hostel since some were not in such good shape to trek both ways. So we got in the van and reached our hostel.

We all got off and a little climb was still there to reach our hostel surrounded by trees and hedges on both sides.

we were climbing and Frank was a little behind me. Suddenly he stiffened,and became alert. He took out his torch and flashed it around among the trees

"Let's move fast", he said under his breath, "I have a feeling we are being watched".

Frank had felt the hair on his neck rise. He had sensed danger. His animal instincts had warned him of the presence of someone.

He had not wanted to scare Geeta. He had seen her safely to her room and then retreated to his. The attraction he had felt for Geeta had increased tenfold along with his protective feelings. Who was the person at the base? Was he there for Geeta or someone else? He had to find out. He decided to take a look in the morning. It was time to rest now. A night's sleep always sharpened one's mind. As soon as his head hit the pillow sleep overtook him. When he woke up it was early morning and the sun was rising Last night he had dreamt of Sheena after a long time. She had come in his dreams. When he had approached her, her face had been of Geeta's. Maybe because he had been thinking about the two of them, his subconscious had muddled them and presented them to him in his dreams, he reasoned. But his heart was saying that he was in a danger of a different kind from the beautiful dark eyes that spoke volumes without uttering a word. "Sometimes what subconscious Detects Our mind with reasons rejects"

Chapter 16

We had come back safely to the hostel and retired to our respective rooms. I was dead tired As I readied for bed, my mind kept on wandering towards Frank. I reminded myself several times that once I left this place I would never see him again. As soon as I snuggled under the covers,I was immediately asleep. I was dead to the world.

The nightmare was back again.

I was once again running on a dark road trying to escape from someone but this time I was falling from a cliff.

As I started to fall I woke up with a jerk. Oh God! It always seemed so real. My heart was still doing staccatos, I was wet with perspiration and my throat was parched like I had run a marathon. I took a few gulps of water from my bedside bottle. I was feeling a bit better now.

Why again? Was that Frank's words that triggered my anxiety and nightmare or was it an indication of coming events?

Was my subconscious trying to warn me about something or someone?

For the past few days I had been behaving quite recklessly and out of my character

Otherwise I always believed in keeping a safe distance from everyone.

Suddenly I felt a shadow cross my window - a man's shadow

It was there only for a brief moment but the silhouette was quite clear.

My thoughts started racing at the speed of lightning. Was the man following me? What was he doing outside my window, at this time of the night?

My rational side however reasoned that after all it was a hostel and many guests and staff lived here, so maybe one of them was out on a stroll or errand.

So I decided to check my door and window and then went back to sleep.

I woke up late. The day was clear and bright and the sun was already up. I recalled the previous night's happenings and looked at a message flashing on my mobile. I stiffened.

It read "I am coming for you I know where you are "

There was no name but she knew it was from Tarun. Her sixth sense was telling her that it was him!

Was he the one stalking her last night or had he hired someone else?

But how did he find her number? First it was the mail and now a message.

He had followed her here as well. Now she was sure that he was the man outside her window last night.

Who had tipped him? She started wondering if he had followed her from Delhi.

She had not told anyone where she was going. She was baffled.

Was she being stalked from her house?

Her mind started racing. Was it Sumi or Frank ?

Now she was not so sure of anyone anymore – neither Frank nor Sumi

Was he acting last night?

My heart was not willing to believe it but my mind was telling me to be cautious. If Frank was the culprit then why did he say that he felt someone watching us?

There were some missing pieces in the puzzle. Until they fall into correct places the full picture won't emerge.

I got ready to go down for breakfast. My enthusiasm for last night had ebbed. I had reverted back into my serious mood.
I wanted to study Frank and check if there was really someone outside my window.

When I went down Frank was already in the dining area reading a magazine.
"Good morning ! Did you sleep well?", he asked.
"Morning! Yes", I replied and ordered breakfast.

Frank had sensed a change in her mood
"Are you okay?"
"Yes I am fine. Just a little bit tired I guess", I replied lamely.
"If you say so".
I became busy in peeling the eggs I did not feel like talking much
We were both silent as if we had run out of topics to talk about.
He immersed himself in a newspaper.

"Someone was outside my window last night" I blurted out then bit my tongue cursing myself for my foolishness.

He became alert, "Are you sure ?"

"Yes, on my balcony. Thankfully it was locked from inside. I don't know how long he was there, I just saw his silhouette".

"Let's go and investigate! If he would have jumped from your balcony then he must have left some marks".

I hurriedly finished my breakfast and came out to inspect the lawn under my balcony. There were footprints on the flowerbed but they could have been made by anyone, staff or guests.

We were just trying to act normal and not alert the stalker if he was still present among the guests.

Today we were to visit some tourist spots. Bhagsu Falls, Namgyal Monastery, etc

Many tourists were going on the tour and I wanted to explore too. Sitting here would have given me more anxiety.

Therefore, Frank also decided to accompany me.

An SUV was given to us; two more passengers were with us in our group.

The trip which started with trepidation was now lifting my mood.

I really liked the monastery ; the abode of His Holiness Dalai Lama. I felt a sense of peace here.

We offered a pack of soft drinks, biscuits and chips to Lord Buddha and I bought a singing bowl while returning. It is a bowl with a pestle and when it is rotated inside the bowl, the most beautiful melodious sound comes out of it and resonates for a while.

Bhagsu Falls was beautiful too! We had tea at Shiva Cafe there

The whole day had turned out quite great! I had captured many beautiful moments to relive at leisure.

Now I was tired and the day was ending so we all gathered in our SUV to head back to our hostel.

Our SUV was travelling through the serpentine roads with gorges at one side and mountain on the other and evening was descending

After last night's incidents I had decided to cut my trip short and instead of returning by bus a few days later, I had chosen to fly to Delhi.

Though my booking was for a couple of days more, I just wanted to give the stalker the slip.

We were going at a smooth speed; suddenly our vehicle started to slow and stopped at a side leaving the way for other vehicles to pass. A Flat tyre- we were informed. We all got down and they started the process of changing tyres.

I started pacing around along with the other guests. They too were strolling, having a look at the scenery.

Suddenly I felt a movement behind me. I turned around and all the blood drained from my face.

Tarun.

The man I had been dreading to meet was standing in front of me Smirking.

I was trapped. I had made a grave mistake by taking a stroll around. I was not even visible from where the car stood. Darkness was descending and my hope was to buy some time by engaging him in small talks.

Moonlight was falling on Tarun's face. I could see death in his eyes.

I was damn scared.

But fear can paralyse as well as make you do superhuman tasks.

I don't know what God had thought about me when I had started to hope a bit and now my past was standing in front of me.

"Did you think you could outrun me and hobnob with another man?", Tarun growled.

"You are crazy!" ,I said ,"we are divorced".

"You might think so but I never let anything which had once belonged to me go. I don't like anyone using things of mine I use it or no one else will", he sneered.

"I am not a thing to be used!", I retorted.

"How could you Geeta? You knew me so well, I had warned you Don't do a run-out on me I will chase you to the end of the world".

"What will you gain by killing me?", I asked.

He laughed a menacing laugh.

Oh God! He is a psycho! What did I see in him to fall for!?" I thought.

"Hh...how did you find me?", I stuttered.

"I had you tailed."

"But why? what will you gain? You are free now! You can have other women

'I tried hard to reason while simultaneously trying to back away from him slowly.

"You were always on the dumb side. You are worth a million dead, then alive."

Finally everything clicked into place. The insurance policy he had taken out had him as the nominee. I had completely forgotten.

"I would have got you killed in Karnal. But that godforsaken woman with the gun spoiled my plan".

As if all parts of the puzzle were falling into place, I realized that it was the bakery-woman sitting at the back of the bus who I had seen in the emporium in a local attire. Yes she was the tail!

So easy to track I must have been.

"You seem to have become spoiled after leaving me, have started being too pally with people I see", he paused for a while and then continued, "Who is that guy?"

He lurched forward at me and I backed as if on instinct Turning back , I broke into a run for my life. I was living my nightmare again.

I was running and running and running on the dark road, away from my car, a gorge on one side I felt no sound of feet behind me but I kept on running for my life.

Suddenly I was bathed in light of a motorcycle headlight. He had come riding behind me and was playing cat and mouse with me.

I started running in zig zags,to dodge his speed I saw death coming my way. I was getting tired but the will to live is strong in every life breathing on earth. I couldn't let the devil win. Whatever may come I won't let him win easily! The thought flashed in my mind. I saw a tree ahead ,it was now or never ,I just took a leap of faith and leapt behind it precariously holding onto its branch at the brink of the gorge. It was better taking a risk than die at his hand. My heart was beating so fast I could hear it in my ears.

I could feel the blood pounding in my veins. My face was hot as if burning.

Tarun had not seen this coming. He was coming in full force and tried to veer his bike , to hit me. I believe it was my parents' prayers or some guardian angels who were protecting me that day.

His bike suddenly tripped over a stone and in front of my eyes toppled over into the gorge along with Tarun and in a matter of minutes burst into flames! Leaping tongues of fire could be seen from the top. They were casting an eerie orange light. The smell of burning petrol filled the mountain air. My head was pounding. Everything looked surreal.

I may have hated him but never wished for such a horrible end.

It all happened in a matter of a few minutes but to me it seemed like an eternity.

I came out slowly from behind the tree, my feet felt heavy as if made of stone

I had sunk to my knees and began crying inconsolably. I felt frozen.

My whole body was trembling with shock.

The scene felt as if taken out from a movie but it was real life not reel.

"My baby! my poor baby! Shh! It's over", Frank cooed.

He had come running behind me and witnessed the last scenes from far.

He clasped me in his arms hugging me tight, planting frantic kisses all over my face, like his life depended on it.

"Oh God! if anything would have happened to you it would have been the death of me too!.I love you so much my sweetie. Are you alright?". He was holding me tight to his chest

Other people also came running to the spot. He reluctantly released me from his arms. I was shivering hard

The police had arrived too. In the light of the flames from the bike, the outline of his body was visible.

The police sent people down to check on Tarun. He was dead, he had broken his neck. Maybe he had died an instant death or had the time to repent for his deeds. Who knows!

I was taken to the hospital for a check-up. I told the police whatever had happened and there were many witnesses as well. The doctor told me that I was fine physically apart from a few scratches but mentally I was shaken and may take time to get out of the trauma. Soon I was filled with paradoxical thoughts. Perhaps I was a bit crazy,I felt pity as well as relief at the same time. I was reminiscing all the bittersweet memories I had of him; more bitter than sweet. I literally had seen my own death before my eyes instead of Tarun's. Death had indeed come at a hair-breadth away from me and then instead of taking me had taken Tarun. I was again traversing through that path of trauma and therapy. However, this time I had Frank with me. We had returned back to Delhi by flight a couple of days later and I had rested to restore back my full faculties.

Frank was very caring and attentive. He said that he too was surprised how his proclamation of love had come out. I think it was all a divine plan.

I called Sumi too. She was happy to hear from me and came rushing to my side.

I apprised her of the accident.

"Good Riddance!", she said in a matter-of-fact way. "Don't sympathise with him just because he died a tragic death. He got what he asked for. He was an asshole.

It could easily have been you at the bottom of the gorge".

My parents were concerned but I told them I was doing fine.

The bakery lady was arrested and she had spilled the beans. She was Tarun's girlfriend. Both of them had wanted easy money. He had promised to invest in her bakery shop. How gullible she was! I could understand that Tarun was a con artist and could make you believe that he would buy you the world

This journey had been liberating.

It freed me from my inhibitions and nightmares, made me do things which I could never even have dreamt of doing!

CROSS

Life is sweet as well as gross
Everyone bears his own cross
We stumble on the way
But get up and move
We are strong, trying to prove
Outside whatever we show
Inside what we are, we know
Ravaged by unknown fears
Through murky waters we sail
We do reach the shore for sure
Many, many times we fail

"Everything has an equal and opposite reaction".
This is the rule of nature What Tarun had set out to do to me, he got it back himself and in equal amount He had forgotten that
"Karma is a mean little bitch".

Chapter 17

Sumi was sitting in her room reflecting on the events of the past few days. They had been like no other.

She again picked up her phone and started dialling a number.

A ringing of the bell at the other end could be heard.

It was picked up this time

"Hello", a female voice answered.

"Mom ! How are you?"

"Sumi! my child, how are you? we are good".

"Mom I have to tell you something. I hope you will not judge me and still love me".

A concerned voice answered "Are you okay? Are you ill ? Are you in need of money honey? Have you lost your job!?"

"You know you are always loved. You can come back home. Don't worry about money, my Beboo".

"No no mom, relax, I am fine. Nothing of that sort has happened".
"Then what?"

"That's what I am trying to tell Mom I am not straight, I mean I am lesbian. Do you know what it is ?", she had been blabbering incoherently.

There was silence at the other end.

Sumi realised finally that the cat was out of the bag She had said it out loud and was feeling a bit relieved

"Shut up Sumi! I know what lesbian is. I was not born yesterday.

Are you sure Sumi!?"

"Yes mom I have been this way from the start but I had been hiding my sexuality in a closet. It is up to you to accept or disown me".

"What nonsense are you talking about!? Do you think so little of my love for you? You are our beautiful loving daughter and so you shall remain.It was just the shock I had not expected to hear this and that kept me mum".

Sumi had not expected her mom to be so accepting She started crying over the phone

"Oh mom I would have been so tightly strung had you refused to accept me, my heart would have been broken I thought you too would be like the parents of Harshita. They killed her for being a lesbian".

Sumi was crying and talking and venting out her pain to the deepest bosom on earth , that is, a mother's bosom.

"Don't cry Sumi ,I will come to Delhi to rest your fears. My poor baby has been so much hurt and hiding from me".

Sumi 's mother had broken the news to her father as well. He had taken a little while to assimilate but had accepted. What was created by nature can't be undone. We should not meddle with it. God wanted it to be this way" , he had said His love for his daughter had overcome all his fears and notions.

They had come to meet their daughter in Delhi

With her parents' acceptance and support she had become happier.

They had been helping her to overcome her pain and move on in life and she had started blooming anew ,beginning to reach new career heights.

They had made her believe she was unique

UNIQUE

***U**nusual you are*
***N**ever believe otherwise*
***I**n you are*
***Q**ualities*
***U**ncommon to*
***E**veryone*

Yes ! She was unique indeed.

EPILOGUE

Geeta looked up from her laptop at the man sleeping on her bed and her son next to him. He looked like an exact copy of the man sleeping in repose.

Frank had courted me for a year. I was reluctant to take the plunge of 'I do'. My parents however had approved of him, he had all the points in his favour.

He had served the country. He had a steady business. Was a caring person who had cared for his wife and ailing mother in the past. He knew the value of family.

Above all he had also been a pillar of strength during my trauma and trials and misgivings.

He loved me with all my messy ways and idiosyncrasies.

He would often talk about how lonely he was when there was no one to scatter toys and mess up his bed. He celebrated it. He was a wonderful man with a unique perspective.

He says,

THE MESS

I love a little mess in my life

It gives a little zing

If everything is slotted in its place

No rush to look for misplaced things

Life would be a bit boring

The pleasure of finding an old card or letter at places odd.

It's like finding a treasure.

You stop to read , forgetting what was the matter

A little mess is celebration of life

Only things remain at its place where no life resides.

I love him too with all his insecurities and shortcomings.

We had tied the knot after a year.

Sumi too had been a part of my friend-sphere. She too had moved on with her life and was seeing someone.

She had joined a LGBTQ Club, Frank and me being her constant support. She had pursued Harshit's case and because of her efforts her culprits had been arrested

The horrific crime of honour-killing people from the LGBTQ+ community rocked the nation Her parents are now lodged in jail along with the hired assassins.

When I had announced my pregnancy, Frank had been frantic with worry. With all his misgivings from the past experience, he had gone mad running around the hospital at the time of delivery, more anxious than I had been. When little Rohan was placed in his arms he was elated but more concerned about me.

Our life had come a full circle.

He was very protective of his family, we both had fought our demons to find happiness.

"More difficult is the path you enjoy 'at last'."

Our journey of pain had ended. God had been most kind to us.

After all her troubles and tribulations, Geeta had risen like a phoenix.

SONG OF THE PHOENIX

She was the bird of lyre
Arose from her funeral pyre
Beautiful scarlet golden plumes
In graceful splendour she boomed
When she sang her melodious song
The sun would stop to listen along
Fragrant herbs in her beak
She reached aloft the mountain peak
To build an aromatic nest
To re-morph and take some rest
Her nest became her pyre
But she was made of fire
When everyone thought her dead and done
From ashes she rose as glorious sun
I am a woman don't you take me light
Phoenix I am ,again will rise

The shell in which she and Frank had been living had finally cracked open and the sun was shining all over
Geeta closed her laptop, kissed her sleeping son and went back to lie beside Frank. He mumbled something in his sleep and dragged her into his arms. She thanked God. Her cup was full

www.ingramcontent.com/pod-product-compliance
Ingram Content Group UK Ltd.
Pitfield, Milton Keynes, MK11 3LW, UK
UKHW021647190726
13853UKWH00001B/114

9 789354 275647